CONTENTS

Dedicated to all Michigan teachers of children.

THE LIFE OF ME, PETOSKEY PETE

Written and Illustrated by Lindsay Boone

Photos by Lindsay Boone

Hi, I'm Petoskey Pete!
I'm a rock, and a fascinating one at that.

I am covered in attractive markings and have been chosen as the official state rock of Michigan.

Many have toured the beaches of the beautiful Lake Michigan and have pondered the magnificence of rocks like me.

People have wondered for centuries how Petoskey stones are formed.

Today, I will tell you the facts.

Have you ever heard of a fossil?
Petoskey stones like me are fossils.

Fossils are
the remains of
plants or animals from
prehistoric times.

You see I wasn't always a rock.
Over 350 million years ago, a shallow sea
covered Michigan.

Let's go back in time…

350 Million Years Ago...

Before I was a rock, I was a piece of live coral connected to a colony of coral.

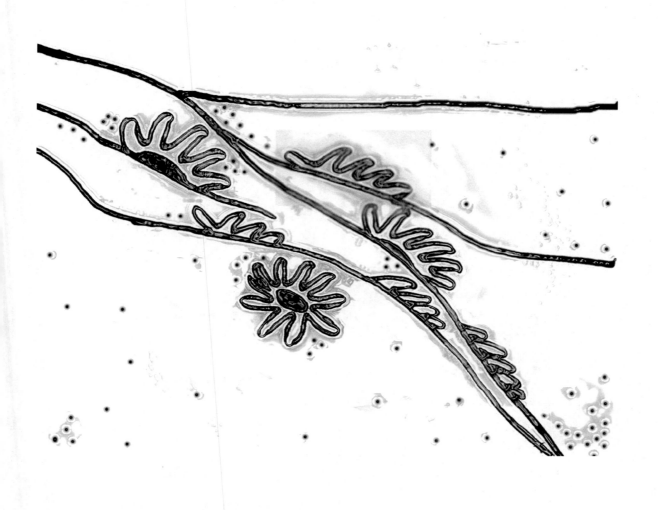

Until an underwater landslide suddenly
covered me!

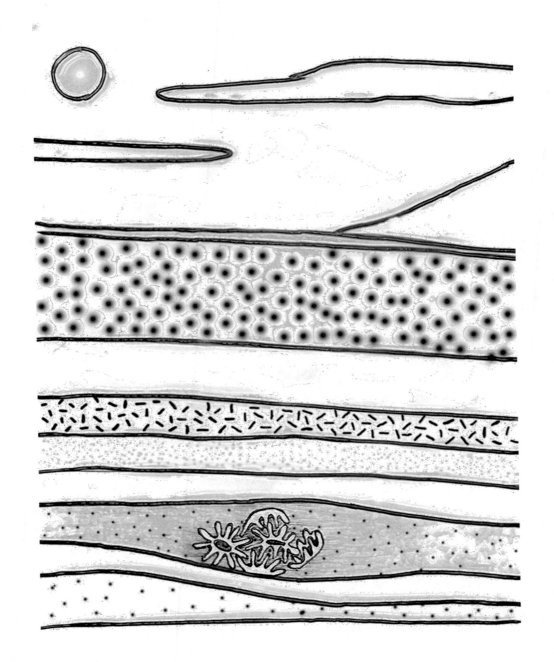

Over thousands of years, I was covered
with layers and layers of mud. That mud
became heavier and heavier, packing tight
around me, rock tight.

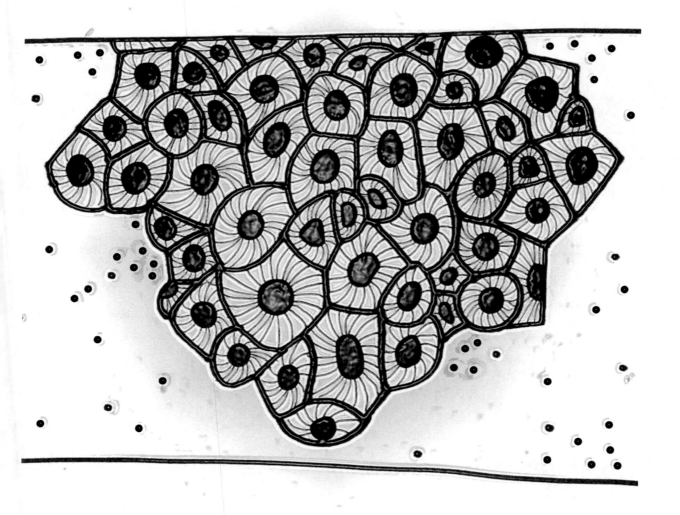

After I was buried for a long time, I began to fossilize. Soon I was a real rock, fossilized in the bedrock.

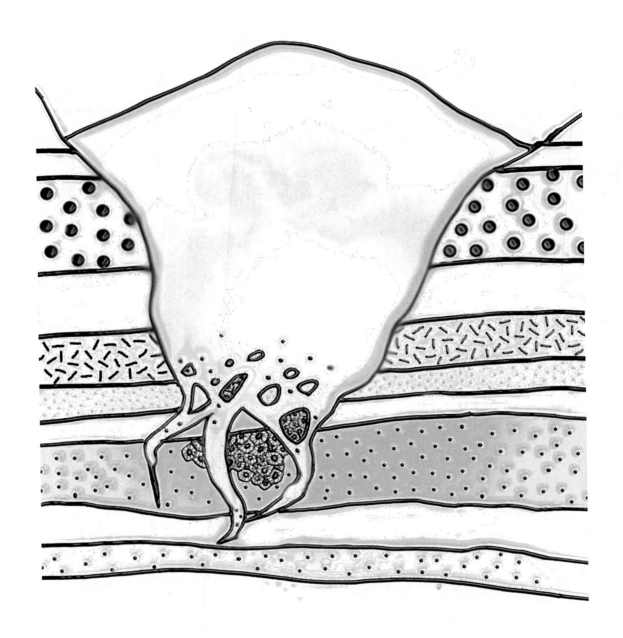

Millions of years later, the Great Lakes
began to form and I was broken free from
the bedrock by the powerful forces of
glaciers.

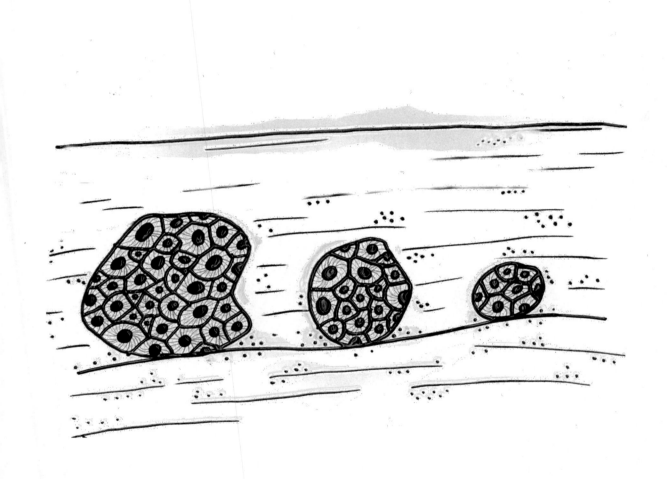

After years and years of rolling on the floor of Lake Michigan and crashing into the beaches, I became the smooth round rock you see today.

Today...

Now you know how I
was formed. Tell your friends and
family about my amazing beauty and
just what a cool rock that I am.

See you next time you visit the scenic
beaches of Lake Michigan!

GLOSSARY

Bedrock – solid rock that lies beneath the soil and has been unaltered by forces of weather.

Fossil – plants or animals, or impressions of them, that have been preserved over time in sedimentary rocks.

Coral – a marine organism.

Colony – a group (in this case, of coral) living or growing close together.

Glaciers – a large mass of ice moving slowly over land.

Sedimentary rock – rocks formed from deposits of sediment, like mud, sand or other rocks.

PETOSKEY STONE Q & A

Why are Petoskey stones found only in the Great Lakes Region?

Petoskey Stones were formed from a coral called Hexagonaria Percarinata. The sea that covered Michigan during the Devonian Period (540 - 350 million years ago) was only about 200 feet deep. That's shallow for a sea. This sea created the perfect environment for that specific type of coral to grow because of how shallow it was. Now we can find fossils of this coral, known as Petoskey stones, across the great state of Michigan.

How did glaciers break up the bedrock?

As glaciers recede, or melt away, the rocks they have picked up as they moved grind the surface of the bedrock like sandpaper. As the seasons change from winter to summer, the water from the melting glaciers seeps into the bedrock. In colder months, it freezes and expands, causing pieces of the bedrock to lift away.

How is a fossil formed?

There are many ways that fossils are formed. Petoskey stones, and other fossils of marine life and plants, are most likely formed by a process called *carbonization*. As a plant or animal is buried in layers and layers of mud, it begins to decompose. The sediment and minerals in the mud that surround the organism slowly replaces its tissue as it breaks down. When the more fragile remains break down, they usually dissolve and are completely removed. What is left is a fossil – a rock that looks kind of like the organism it is preserving.

How did Petoskey stones get their name?

Petoskey Stones are named after the city of Petoskey in Northern Michigan. This area, along the Northern coast of Lake Michigan, is where many Petoskey stones have been found for centuries.

Where can I find a Petoskey stone?

You can find Petoskey stones along the shores of Lake Michigan in Northern Michigan. Petoskey State Park and Antrim County Barnes Park are two great places to start searching. However, you may get lucky and find a Petoskey Stone in road cuts or gravel pits across the state of Michigan.

PETOSKEY PETE SONG

(Sing to a hip-hop beat)

Petoskey Pete, you're so neat
Now we're telling your story to a different beat.

You were a coral but then you died
Covered in mud, there you lie.

Millions of years went by
The mud packed tight and you fossilized.

Pete, Pete, Petoskey Pete
We're telling your story to a different beat.

In bedrock there you stayed
Until glaciers came and eroded you away.

Soon there was a great big lake
The waves sanded you smooth, make no mistake.

Pete, Pete, Petoskey Pete
We've told your story to a different beat.

(Words by Lindsay Boone)

PETOSKEY PETE QUIZ

Name _Junia_ Date _10-12-9_

1. Where are Petoskey stones found?

   michigghn

2. What were Petoskey stones before they
   fossilized? _Coll_

3. How long ago was Michigan covered by a shallow
   sea? _350 Millon yeas a go_

4. How did Petoskey stones become so smooth?

   mud

5. How were the Petoskey stone fossils broken free
   from the bedrock?

   Geysers

EXTRA CREDIT:

What is a fossil?

a Fossil is Something that
was Coverd by mud and
the mud will cover it For 200 to 300
yaers long then thay are fossils

Permission to copy for educational purposes.

PETOSKEY STONE LEARNING ACTIVITIES

Lessons
about Petoskey stones
incorporating most learning styles
at various grade levels

PETOSKEY STONE SEARCH

MATERIALS:

- Internet access – one computer per learner or group of two learners
- Petoskey Stone Search worksheet – one per learner or group of two learners

Learners will use their Internet searching skills to look up the answers to scientific questions on a worksheet while working in small groups or individually.

Procedure:

- The learners should understand how to use Internet search engines and the rules and behavior you expect from them while searching online.
- The learners can work together in groups of two or individually to complete the worksheet by searching for the answers on the Internet. They will use the words in **BOLD** to help them search.
- The learners will also keep a record of where they found the information by writing down the website in the space provided.
- The teacher will review the answers with the class when they have completed the worksheet.

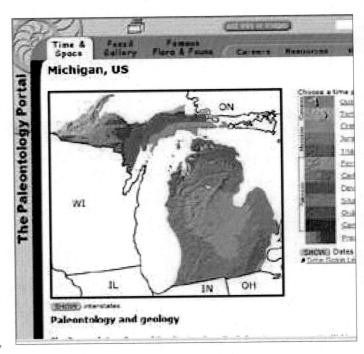

Source: www.paleoportal.org

PETOSKEY STONE SEARCH

Name(s)_____

DIRECTIONS: Search the Internet to answer the following questions. Use the bold words to help you search. Remember to write the name of the website where you found the answers in the space provided.

1. 350 Million years ago, when a shallow sea covered Michigan, is often referred to as "**the age of fish**." What is the actual name for this time period?

   _____

   website: _____

2. Approximately how **deep** was the **sea** that **covered Michigan** during this time?

   _____

   website: _____

3. Briefly describe how **glaciers carved** the **lakes of Michigan**, exposing the Petoskey stone fossils? _____

   _____

   _____

   website: _____

4. When did **glaciers cover Michigan** and break up the bedrock full of Petoskey stone fossils?_____

   website: _____

5. What is the **scientific name for Petoskey stones**?

   _____

   website: _____

PETOSKEY QUESTION BOX

MATERIALS:
- Box making worksheet - one per two learners
- Scissors – one per two learners
- Colored pencils – one box per two learners
- Scotch tape – seven 1.5 inch pieces per two learners

Learners will work together to create a box with questions about Petoskey stones. They will share their boxes with other classmates to quiz each other on their knowledge of Petoskey Stones.

Procedure:

- The learners will work in pairs of two and create a list of six questions and answers based on their knowledge of Petoskey stones.
- The pairs will write their questions on the box making worksheet using their colored pencils.
- The learners will work together to cut out and assemble their boxes following directions on the box making worksheet.
- Each group of two will then partner with another group of two and share their boxes by taking turns rolling the them like dice and answering each other's questions.

PETOSKEY QUESTION BOX

BOX MAKING TEMPLATE

DIRECTIONS:
1. Write one question in each square
2. Cut along the solid lines
3. Fold on the dotted lines to form a box
4. Tape the edges together

PETOSKEY STONE TIMELINE

MATERIALS:
- Petoskey Stone Timeline Learner worksheet
- Colored pencils or crayons for each learner

During this activity, the learners will be using their knowledge of Petoskey stones in order to draw and label a timeline of the formation of Petoskey Stones.

Procedure:
- The learners will work individually to draw, chronologically, the stages of the formation of Petoskey stones.
- The learners will label their drawings to demonstrate their knowledge of the formation of Petoskey stones.

Alternate art activity:
The black and white pages of this book (where Petoskey Pete describes his formation) can be photo copied and made into a coloring book for each learner.

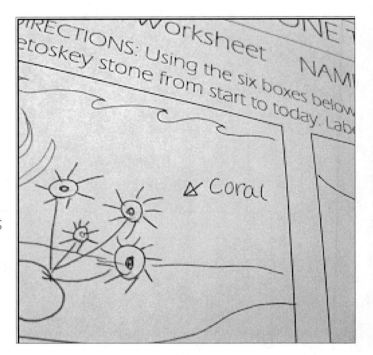

PETOSKEY STONE TIMELINE

Learner Worksheet   NAME: _____

DIRECTIONS: Using the six boxes below, draw the stages of the life of a Petoskey stone from coral to today. Label your drawings.

DEAR PETOSKEY PETE

MATERIALS:
- Petoskey Pete Letter Worksheet – one per learner
- One rock per learner – any size or type of rock (optional)

Learners will write a letter to Petoskey Pete after reading his story using their knowledge of letter writing and the formation of Petoskey stones.

Procedure:

- Learners should know the format of a letter. For example, they should know to start the letter with "Dear Petoskey Pete," and end it with something like, "Your Friend, (learner name)."
- The teacher will pass the rocks out to students along with the Petoskey Pete Letter Worksheet and describe the prompt.

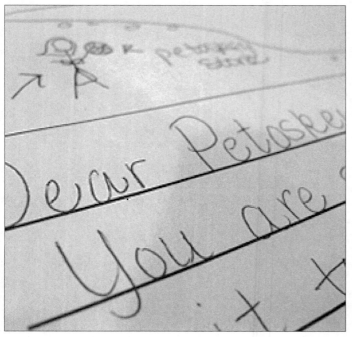

Prompt: The learners will imagine they are the rock they have been given. They will write a letter to Petoskey Pete to convince him to be their friend. Why do they want to be his friend? What is so special about him? etc.

Other Optional Prompts:

- Share about a time you found or saw a Petoskey stone, or about someone you know who has.
- What do you think about Petoskey Pete?
- What did you learn from reading about Petoskey Pete?
- Have you ever looked for a Petoskey Stone or do you want to now?
- Open response to the story.

DEAR PETOSKEY PETE

_____,

_____

_____

_____

_____

_____

_____

_____

PETOSKEY CHARADES

MATERIALS:
- Petoskey Charades Cards, one per group (six groups total)

Learners will divide into groups and play a charades-like game of pantomiming the steps of the formation of Petoskey stones.

Procedure:

- The teacher will cut out each card from the Petoskey Charades Cards handout.
- The teacher will divide the class into six groups and explain the directions to the Petoskey Charades activity.
- The teacher will hand out one card per group
- The learners will work together to figure out how they plan to pantomime their part of Petoskey stone formation as indicated on their group's card.
- The teacher will then call random groups (try not to call in formation order) to present their pantomime performance in front of the class (no talking).
- After watching each group, the rest of the class will try to guess what portion of the formation that group is performing.
- As the class guesses correctly, one representative from each group will stand aside holding up their group's card.
- As each group's performance is guessed, the learners will organize the cards in chronological order until each group has performed and all cards are being held by the representatives in the correct order.
- The teacher will review the formation of Petoskey stones by reading through the cards being held by group members.

PETOSKEY CHARADES CARDS

Coral living over 350 million years ago.

A landslide covers the coral.

Layers and layers of mud cover the coral.

Fossilizing coral stuck in the mud.

Fossil being dug up by a glacier.

Petoskey stones rolling smooth on the lake's floor.

HEXAGON WATERCOLOR

MATERIALS:
- Watercolor paper, one sheet per learner
- Templates of Hexagons, one per learner (about 3 inches wide)
- One white crayon per learner
- Pieces of sponge, two per learner
- Watercolors - various shades of brown, tan and gray for all learners.
- Scissors, one pair per learner

Petoskey stones are also known as Hexagonoria (six sided), so this piece of artwork the students will create will look like a Petoskey stone and will use hexagon templates and tessellations in the process.

Procedure:
- The teacher will demonstrate the artwork step by step as the learners work.
- The learners will begin by tracing their hexagon templates on the watercolor paper with the white crayons. They will trace in a pattern, where the edges of the hexagons all meet together (tessellations). Be sure to press the crayon hard and go over the template pattern a few times to ensure the line is nice and thick (the crayon wax will not allow the watercolor to stain the paper, but if the line is not thick enough, some color may leak through and the result will not be as vivid and clear).

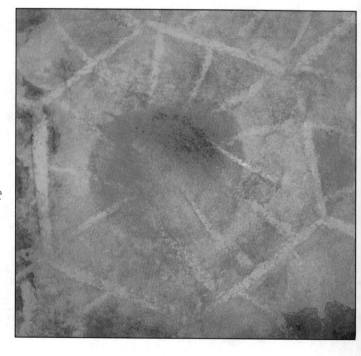

HEXAGON WATERCOLOR

The learners will use their crayon to make lighter lines going toward the center of each hexagon, but not meeting in the middle (leave a blank spot in the center for the dark 'mouth' of the Petoskey stones).

The learners will use a sponge and the brown and tan shades of watercolor to completely cover the entire paper (the shades should have variation, but the entire paper should be covered, with exception of the white crayon lines).

The learners will use the other sponge to put the dark spots ('mouths') of the Petoskey stones in the center of each hexagon shape.

Once the watercolor dries, the learners will cut their paper into a 'rock' shape. Each learner will have one large Petoskey stone watercolor.

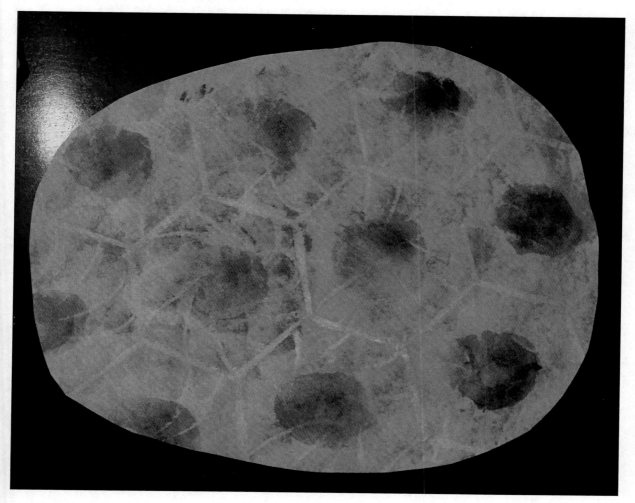

OUR STATE SYMBOLS

MATERIALS:

- Internet access – one computer per learner or group of two learners
- Our State Symbols worksheet – one per learner

Learners will search the Internet for a website to help them find some of Michigan's state symbols, including our state bird, flower, tree and more.

Procedure:

- The learners should understand how to use Internet search engines and the rules and behavior you expect from them while searching online.
- The learners will search for "Michigan state symbols" using an Internet search engine.
- The learners will complete their worksheets and draw a picture of the state flag in the space provided.
- The teacher will review the answers with the class when they have completed the worksheet.

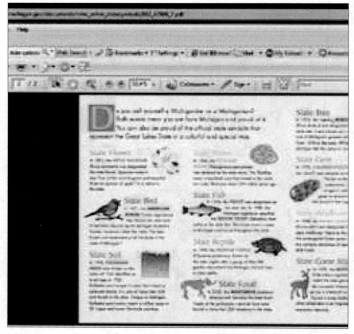

Source: www.michigan.gov

OUR STATE SYMBOLS

Name: _____

Using an Internet search engine, search for
"Michigan state symbols."
Find a site that will help you fill in the blanks below.

Michigan's state mammal is the _____.

Michigan's state stone is the _____.

Michigan's state flower is the _____.

Michigan's state bird is the _____.

Michigan's state fish is the _____.

Michigan's state tree is the _____.

Draw a picture of our state flag in the box below:

PETOSKEY STONE NOTES

PETOSKEY STONE NOTES

References

Note: The information in this book regarding the formation of Petoskey Stones was derived from the following sources:

Mueller, Bruce and William H. Wilde. (2004). <u>The Complete Guide to Petoskey Stones</u>. Ann Arbor, MI: The University of Michigan Press and Petoskey, MI: The Petoskey Publishing Company.

Michigan Department of Environmental Quality, Geological Survey Division. <u>The Petoskey Stone: Some History, Lore and Facts about the "Petoskey Stone"</u>. <http://www.michigan.gov/documents/deq/ogs-gimdl-GGPS_263213_7.pdf>

Made in the USA
San Bernardino, CA
21 October 2016